Wellington and Kevin are looking at the rain.

Splish, splash, splosh. Rain comes into the kennel.

Flash! Crash! Bang!
Kevin is afraid.
Flash! Crash! Bang!

The puddle gets bigger and bigger. Flash! Crash! Bang!

The water gets deeper and deeper. Flash! Crash! Bang!

Wellington and Kevin have to swim out of the kennel.

They swim to a bank and get out of the water.

Then the rain stops. Wellington and Kevin see a rainbow.